READING SYSTEM

STUDENT WORKBOOK SIX A

THIRD EDITION

by Barbara A. Wilson

Wilson Language Training
175 West Main Street
Millbury, Massachusetts 01527-1915
(508) 865-5699

ISBN 1-56778-087-3	Student Workbook Six A	Item# SW6A
ISBN 1-56778-080-6	Student Workbooks 1-6 A	Item# WRW16A
ISBN 1-56778-079-2	Student Workbooks 1-12 A	Item# WRW12A

The Wilson Reading System is published by:

Wilson Language Training Corp.
175 West Main Street
Millbury, MA 01527-1915

Copyright ©1996 Barbara A. Wilson. All rights reserved. No part of this book may be reproduced or utilized in any form or by any electronic or mechanical means, including photocopying, without permission in writing from the author.

Printed in the U.S.A.

Read each suffix below.

en	ness	ful
ment	ly	er
ish	ive	ty
est	es	less
able	y	ing

Copy the suffix endings from above into the correct columns.

vowel suffixes		**consonant suffixes**
__________	__________	__________
__________	__________	__________
__________	__________	__________
__________	__________	__________
	__________	__________
		__________

Read the baseword. Select a suffix from the box at the top of the column to add to the baseword. Write the suffix and then the word on the lines provided. If more than one suffix works, select one.

ish	ing	er
est	y	ive

baby + _____ = ____________

lump + _____ = ____________

wild + _____ = ____________

dress + _____ = ____________

crunch+_____ = ____________

luck +_____ = ____________

publish+____ = ____________

blast + _____ = ____________

fast + _____ = ____________

pink + _____ = ____________

ment	ness	ful
less	ly	ty

hope + _____ = ____________

equip + _____ = ____________

safe + _____ = ____________

respect+_____ = ____________

kind + _____ = ____________

late +_____ = ____________

require+______= ____________

ship + _____ = ____________

hand + _____ = ____________

nine + _____ = ____________

Select a suffix from the top of each box to form a real word. Write the suffix on the line.

ty ly ment	ive ment able
ship ______	protect ______
strong ______	depend ______
six ______	amuse ______

ful er y	ful ness ing
fast ______	spell ______
thank ______	kind ______
grump ______	plate ______

Write the words above on the lines below. Read the words.

______________________ ______________________

______________________ ______________________

______________________ ______________________

______________________ ______________________

______________________ ______________________

______________________ ______________________

Underline or 'scoop' the syllables in the baseword and circle the suffix in each word below. Read the words.

momently	lumpy	freshen
kindness	milder	lateness
silently	thankful	punishing
crunches	childish	lucky
frequently	stronger	trustful
quickly	crunchy	amazement
stinger	secretly	destructive
spending	strongest	brushes
equipment	safety	amusement
dependable	shyness	useless

List words with vowel suffixes from the previous page (4).

consonant suffixes

List words with consonant suffixes from the previous page (4).

vowel suffixes

Read the sentence. Select the correct word from the box to complete the sentence. Write the word on the line. Reread the completed sentence. Use each word in the box only once.

taxes	splashes	sixty	benches	quickly
handful	lonely	difficulty	useful	amusement

1. Sonya felt _____________ when the kids left home.

2. Sid _____________ me with the hose.

3. The kids like to go on all the fast _______________ rides.

4. I had _______________ with this math quiz.

5. The _____________ at the game were cold and damp.

6. My uncle will be ______________ next month.

7. Dad is grumpy when he prepares the ______________ .

8. I will grab a ______________ of nuts for a snack.

9. Dominic runs more ______________ than the rest of the children.

10. Try to find a ___________ gift for Dad.

Underline or "scoop" the syllables in the baseword and circle the suffix. Write the 2 parts on the lines provided. e.g. in spect(ing)= inspect + ing

		baseword		suffix			baseword		suffix
thankful	=	______	+	______	dependable	=	______	+	______
publisher	=	______	+	______	mildest	=	______	+	______
frequently	=	______	+	______	slyly	=	______	+	______
selfish	=	______	+	______	freshen	=	______	+	______
longest	=	______	+	______	destructive	=	______	+	______
hopeless	=	______	+	______	amazement	=	______	+	______
secretly	=	______	+	______	silently	=	______	+	______
kindness	=	______	+	______	expanding	=	______	+	______
strongly	=	______	+	______	crunchy	=	______	+	______
statement	=	______	+	______	taller	=	______	+	______

Write as many suffixes from memory as possible into the correct columns. Then, use your Rules Notebook to fill in any suffixes.

vowel suffixes		**consonant suffixes**

Use each word below in a sentence on the lines provided below. Be sure to start each sentence with a capital letter and end each sentence with punctuation. Proofread carefully.

1. thankful

2. lately

3. equipment

4. strongest

5. wishing

Read each sentence. Underline the basewords and circle the suffixes.

1. Dad protected the small pup from the cold.
2. Sally insulted Sam and disrupted the class.
3. The trash can is infested with insects.
4. Kendra insisted that we stop crying.
5. The talented child will go to the contest.

Read each setence. Cover it. Write it on the line. Uncover it and proofread.

1. ______________________________

____

2. ______________________________

____

3. ______________________________

____

4. ______________________________

____

5. ______________________________

____

"What does the -ed suffix say in each word above?" /___ /

Read each sentence. Underline the basewords and circle the suffixes.

1. Ken was late, but he still wished to visit his dad.
2. The kids camped next to a small pond.
3. Steve dressed himself the moment he awoke.
4. Bill refreshed himself in the cold pond.
5. Wendy limped for quite awhile.

Read each setence. Cover it. Write it on the line. Uncover it and proofread.

1. ____

   ____

2. ____

   ____

3. ____

   ____

4. ____

   ____

5. ____

   ____

"What does the -ed suffix say in each word above?" / ___ /

Underline the baseword and circle the suffix in each word below. Read the word. Write /t/, /d/, or /ed/ above the suffix to indicate the sound.

responded	stamped	happened
requested	expressed	thrilled
neglected	impressed	distracted
complimented	called	trashed
demolished	crunched	depended
defended	winked	banged

Write the ed words in the correct column below.

ed = /ĕd/	**ed** = /d/	**ed** = /t/
____________	____________	____________
____________	____________	____________
____________	____________	____________
____________	____________	____________
____________		____________
____________		____________
____________		____________

Add the suffix to each baseword. Above the <u>ed</u> , indicate the sound: /ed/, /d/, /t/.

happen+ed= ________________	insult + ed = ________________
thrill + ed = ________________	belong +ed = ________________
cross + ed = ________________	smell + ed = ________________
expect+ ed = ________________	drench+ed = ________________
connect+ed= ________________	stash + ed = ________________
twist+ed = ________________	intend+ ed = ________________
finish+ed = ________________	bang + ed = ________________
risk + ed = ________________	dump+ ed = ________________
chomp+ed = ________________	skill + ed = ________________
predict+ed = ________________	protect+ed = ________________

Copy the words from the previous page (12) into the correct columns below.

-**ed** = / ed/	-**ed** = /d/	-**ed** = /t/

Select one word from each group above to use in a sentence. Write the sentences below. Proofread careully.

1\. 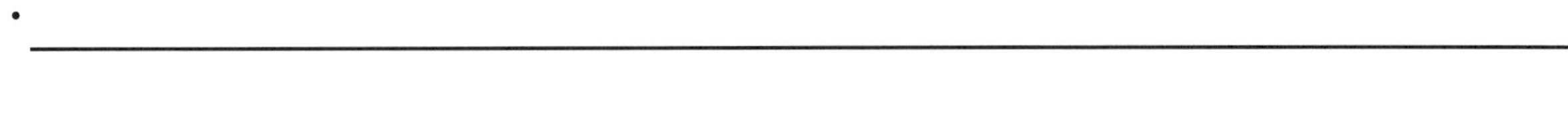

2\. 

3\. 

Read the sentence. Select the correct word from the box to complete the sentence. Write the word on the line. Reread the completed sentence. Use each word in the box only once.

drenched	limped	requested
expected	spilled	

1. Steve _____________ up the steps with his broken leg.
2. The tot _____________ the milk on the basement rug.
3. Mr. Bantam _____________ Dave to win the top prize in the contest.
4. Pam was _____________ *after* the kids tossed her in the lake.

Write the ed word from each sentence on the line. Then choose the sound of ed (/ĕd/, /d/ or /t/).

/ĕd/, /d/ or /t/

1. ______________________ ed says /_____ /
2. ______________________ ed says /_____ /
3. ______________________ ed says /_____ /
4. ______________________ ed says /_____ /
5. ______________________ ed says /_____ /

Find all the suffixes in the sentences below. Underline the basewords and circle the suffixes.

1. It is quite impressive that Steve ranked fifth in the difficult contest.

2. Dad punished the kids when they were disrespectful.

3. The tot clenched his fists on the fast amusement ride.

4. Sam munched on lunch while Jake kindly helped his mom.

5. Anna silently sat while the dentist drilled.

Write the words with suffixes from each sentence on the lines below.

1. __________ __________

2. __________ __________ __________

3. __________ __________ __________

4. __________ __________ __________

5. __________ __________

Combine the basewords and suffixes into words and write them on the lines.

care+less+ly = ______________________

destruct+ive+ly = ______________________

thank+ful+ly = ______________________

use+ful+ly = ______________________

impress+ive+ly = ______________________

respect+ful+ly = ______________________

end+less+ly = ______________________

care+less+ness = ______________________

hope+less+ly = ______________________

help+ful+ly = ______________________

will+ing+ness = ______________________

protect+ive+ly = ______________________

Select a suffix from the top of each box to form a real word. Write the suffix on the line.

less	**ly**	**ive**
use________ly		
act________ly		
trustful______		

ive	**less**	**ly**
care_______ness		
thankful______		
impress______ly		

ful	**ive**	**ly**
respect_____ y		
effective______		
protect_____ly		

ness	**ful**	**ing**
helpful______		
wish_______ly		
will________ly		

Write the words above on the lines below. Read the words.

____________________ ____________________

____________________ ____________________

____________________ ____________________

____________________ ____________________

____________________ ____________________

____________________ ____________________

Read the words. Write the baseword and suffixes on the lines.

	Baseword	+ suffix	+ suffix
uselessly =	________	________	________
skillfully =	________	________	________
lifelessly =	________	________	________
restlessness =	________	________	________
impressively =	________	________	________
destructively =	________	________	________
respectfully =	________	________	________
hopefully =	________	________	________
willingness =	________	________	________
zestfully =	________	________	________

Proofread each sentence. Correct the spelling of the underlined words. Rewrite the sentence on the lines provided. Add capital letters and punctuation.

1. hopefuly we can go on the amusement rid

2. did james carelessle drop the glas vase

3. the class respektfully folded the flag

4. sandra willinly helpt mrs chang

5. kim skilfully hit the basebal

Underline or "scoop" the syllables in the baseword. Circle (separately) the 2 suffixes in each word.
e.g. <u>im</u> <u>press</u> (ive) (ly)

impressively	hopefully	protectively
respectfully	helpfully	willingly
zestfully	carelessly	skillfully
helpfulness	usefulness	wishfulness
restlessly	thankfully	actively

Write the basewords on the lines below.

________________	________________	________________
________________	________________	________________
________________	________________	________________
________________	________________	________________
________________	________________	________________

Find all the words with suffixes. Some will have one suffix; others will have two. Underline the baseword and circle the suffix(es). If there is more than one suffix, circle each suffix separately.

1. rob willingly went to complete the task

2. teddy went in to take a nap, but he tossed restlessly in the bed

3. mom expressively thanked the kids for their helpfulness

4. betsy awoke and gratefully thanked her husband for doing the dishes

5. hopefully, crunchy candy is still in the dish

Write the sentences from above on the lines below. Add capital letters and punctuation. Proofread carefully.

1. ____

____

2. ____

____

3. ____

____

4. ____

____

5. ____

____

Read the words. Write syllables on the lines. Mark the syllables. Mark the vowels.
e.g. bū gle
o cle

bugle	=	______	______	trample	=	______	______
sample	=	______	______	staple	=	______	______
puzzle	=	______	______	grumble	=	______	______
thimble	=	______	______	fable	=	______	______
ripple	=	______	______	cradle	=	______	______
cable	=	______	______	razzle	=	______	______
fiddle	=	______	______	cattle	=	______	______
battle	=	______	______	struggle	=	______	______
stable	=	______	______	able	=	______	______
bottle	=	______	______	title	=	______	______

Read the sentences. Find the words with a consonant-le syllable.
Circle them and then divide the words by underlining or "scooping" each syllable.

1. The club must have a raffle and, hopefully, make some cash.

2. Did the kids struggle with the puzzle?

3. Could you staple these tests and pass them to the kids in class?

4. Jake attempted to juggle with eggs!

5. We must try to get the opponent to fumble the ball.

6. Henry will get the bundle in the van and put it in the pantry.

7. I will sit in the *pony's* saddle.

8. Do not disrupt the baby in the cradle.

9. This is a simple spelling quiz.

10. The bottle is empty, but the baby is still

!@#$%

Underline or "scoop" the syllables in the nonsense words below. Mark the syllable types (c=closed, o=open, c-le= consonant-le). Mark the vowels and read the nonsense syllables.

driggle	plondle	bozzle
ploble	chomdle	weggle
thumple	blittle	shrungle
priffle	muzle	flotle
stodle	spinkle	cheple
shubble	trinzle	strople
thofle	pudle	zingle
brentle	grunzle	blefle
fitle	shobble	chentle
flidle	bopple	fubble

Read the syllables on each side of the box. Draw a line to connect syllables to form real words.

bu	ple
dim	gle
jum	ble

trem	gle
hud	ble
jug	dle

fa	dle
puz	ble
fid	zle

cat	ble
ta	tle
jun	gle

Write the words above on the lines below. Read the words.

______________________ ______________________

______________________ ______________________

______________________ ______________________

______________________ ______________________

______________________ ______________________

______________________ ______________________

Underline or "scoop" the syllables in each word. Cross out the silent e in consonant-le syllables. Find 3 consonant-le syllable exceptions and cross out the silent t. Read the words.

bugle	gobble	fumble
castle	tickle	bundle
staple	tumble	scramble
razzle	tattle	candle
pickle	hustle	table
riddle	drizzle	pebble
jingle	dimple	freckle
dribble	puzzle	raffle
juggle	rifle	buckle
thimble	sample	whistle

REVIEW- Mark the vowels.

__gle	he	fame	__dle
think	clap	shy	crave
pro	try	ill	__zle
stone	__ble	hi	bring
__ple	thump	flake	shade

List the syllables above in the correct column below.

closed:

____

____

____

____

____

vowel-consonant-e

____

____

____

____

____

open:

____

____

____

____

____

consonant-le:

____

____

____

____

____

REVIEW- Use the Syllable Section in Student's Notebook.

Find and circle the syllable exceptions in the words below.

closed: ild, old, olt, ost, ind	**open: a and i**
vowel-consonant-e: ive	**consonant-le: stle**

wild	ago	have
host	whistle	Atlanta
hesitate	give	across
blind	bold	olive
hustle	active	confident
expensive	colt	castle

Write the words above in the correct columns below.

Exceptions

closed

____

____

____

____

____

vowel-consonant-e

____

____

____

____

____

open

____

____

____

____

____

consonant-le

____

____

____

Vocabulary Practice:
Create sentences that include the vocabulary words below. Use a dictionary or electronic spell checker as needed. Underline or "scoop" each syllable in the vocabulary words below.

6.1	**6.2**	**6.3**	**6.4**
frequently	stalled	hopelessly	riddle
dependable	drenched	carelessly	fumble
requirement	lasted	hopefully	struggle
statement	refreshed	carefully	hustle
refreshment	thrilled	willingly	tackle
quickest	clenched	respectfully	handle
amazement	published	actively	sprinkle
kindness	filmed	wishfully	scramble
thankful	requested	helpfully	cuddle
secretly	demolished	skillfully	hobble

Story Starter:
At the end of Step 6 create a story that includes many (at least 5) of the vocabulary words below. This story is about someone helping someone else. Underline each vocabulary word used from the list below.

kindly	finished	struggle	accomplishment
silently	wished	lazy	settle
dependable	hesitate	alone	puzzle
expecting	strongest	longed	frequently
thankful		hopefully	willingly